# EMOTIONS ON TRIAL:

## Science and the Bible Reveal

# EMOTIONS ON TRIAL: SCIENCE AND THE BIBLE REVEAL

By FELIX HAWK

*Cover Design* Evoque Publishing

---

*Interior Design* Evoque Publishing

---

*Publisher* Evoque Publishing

---

*Editor* Daphne Rhea T. Planca

---

1. Religion & Spirituality
2. Spirituality
3. Personal Growth
4. Spiritual Healing
5. Healing.

First Edition
Printed in London, United Kingdom

# Table of Contents

# Introduction

A funny thing about emotions is that they can become addictive. Literally, all our emotions, from euphoria to depression, depend on the proteins segregated by our hypothalamus, a region in the lower brain area. Such proteins enter our blood stream and communicate the intended effect to EACH AND EVERY ONE of the cells we are made of. But the most astonishing aspect of the whole process is that the cell's receptors in charge of processing those proteins are the ones in charge of processing other substances like, for example, heroine.

So affirming that a person can be addicted to a certain emotion (i.e., to the substance associated with that emotion) is certainly more than a metaphor. And, as our biological mechanism involved is the same that deals with drugs, the laws of addiction are here applicable too: under sustained exposure to a substance, the cell becomes more receptive to it, and as it gets more and more into the habit, it will require growing amounts of the same substance simply to recover its balance. Translated into the world of emotions, the same emotion will be more intense and will last for a longer period of time before the cell gets satisfied to the full.

## What This Book Covers

The nature of addictions

Addiction can be described as any behavior that regardless of being prejudicial for the subject (and he being aware of it), he decides to maintain (you can find the canonical definition here). In short, it could also be defined as "something that you cannot stop." Such definition is especially suitable when thinking about emotions.

Emotions themselves are not the problem. They occur for one reason. In many cases, they achieve adaptive purposes, and even when they do not, they are a beautiful, overwhelming manifestation of the nature's capability for variation. Life would be dull without emotions. The problem comes when one of them becomes too "sticky" or, expressing it from the other side of the equation, when we cling too much to it. As I mentioned above, emotional messages are transferred to our whole body, cell-by-cell, so resisting to them has global and sometimes devastating effects.

To make things even worse, western culture has always been more interested in the "outer" aspect of things than in our inner world, so its approach to the field of emotions has been typically limited to a very superficial acknowledgment of its bodily expressions (smile and tear). There seems to exist some kind of taboo on the issue, as if discussing emotions that we all have were a thing of bad taste. Sadly, the invisible nature of feelings makes them easy to ignore … but God helps you with the side effects if you do so.

So how to determine if we suffer an emotional addiction? From self-pity to rage, from systematic pessimism to an exhausting feeling of being irreplaceable … it could be anything. But how to identify it, especially after, in some cases, many years of promoting the wrong neural connections? The previous definition is good as a rule of thumb: if you cannot stop it, then you are addicted. Needless to say, it requires courage and honesty to oneself to find out what is wrong. But the benefits can be huge, too. Real, intimate self-knowledge starts here.

A useful technique: Visualizing the storm

Words are a powerful tool, and a lot of psychological techniques make use of them: to establish time-out periods, to encourage right behaviors, and to improve self-esteem… Invaluable as they are, these techniques also present a drawback that we must take note: every word is like the top of an iceberg, with 90 percent of its mass being its underlying connotations, which vary from every person, is thus impossible to control and can have strong effects on the results. Besides, the nature of language itself, and our everyday "overuse" of it, makes it difficult to distance oneself from words, a distance particularly important when dealing with emotions. That is why, generally speaking, visual techniques are more effective than verbal ones when dealing with emotions, although it is also important to remark that as configuration and abilities differ from brain to brain, one person can be more naturally inclined to verbal or visual techniques, depending on his most developed areas. "Visualizing the storm" is what I call to a technique that I have found really useful to monitor and become more aware of emotions.

Imagine your own brain. Visualize it. At the same time, feel it there, with you, being you in fact. Feel its round 3 lb somewhere up there. It is important that you do both things, visualizing and feeling, because every stimulus that enters our consciousness by several simultaneous channels multiplies its efficiency.

Emotions are not ghosts; they are flows of proteins unchained by electric signals in our brain, which, in its turn, waits for the reaction to generate new signals, etc. So whenever you experiment an overwhelming emotion of any kind, focus on your brain. It is all there. Imagine the surface. Focus on the electric discharges going from one point to another. Bzz! There goes another. Take a step back from your emotions, try to see them as something that happens to you, like hiccups. Take a deep breath. Visualize the storm, all those tiny blue rays twisting, flashing, communicating two points for an instant, and starting the new protein discharge. Feel the protein flow as it goes down your spine, flows through your blood, feeds your cells, all of your cells. You are the one who has that weird electrical crown in his head. No problem. Be open to the sensation, just let it come, and associate it with the image of your brain, just as if you were watching a fascinating documentary on your brain. Keep yourself separated from what you feel, you did not ask that protein to come in, but now it is here, so just watch how it flows, spreads, dissolves, and then leaves room for a different thing.

In any situation in your life, you always have the option to decide what "is you" and what simply "happens to you." It is you who name it, you who set the line. The healthiest thing to do in this case is to detach. It feels weird when you start, but once you get used to it, it feels literal and natural, like taking a huge weight off your shoulders. This stance is similar to what Buddhists call "detachment." You do not give up your feelings, but you do not grab them either.

A great advantage of this technique is that as you get better at visualizing, you will start to see others as "victims" of their own protein addictions too. By no means, it exempts them from responsibility for their actions: it is their obligation to modify such protein habits. But this radical change of focus can make you more open and compassionate toward other people. Moving from seeing someone as a menace, for example, to consider him a poor lad, momentarily "fried" by his own brain, is a radical turn, and it will help you to deal with problems more effectively and with lower energy consumption. Besides, a more compassionate stance is certainly perceived by the others; it generates positive feedback which in turn, etc.

Limitations: monotony always reduces effectiveness, that is a universal law. Seemingly, our nervous system gets bored with any repetition of stimuli and then starts to lose interest. This is called the law of fatigue. Once your mind becomes "fed up" with this visualization, do not force it. You better have a rest, move on a different matter, and let the system get "clean." The brain is still very mysterious that it is tough to tell for sure, but it would also be a good idea maybe to move to a verbal activity for a while to exercise a different brain area.

Thanks for downloading this book. It is my firm belief that it will provide you with all of the answers to your questions.

# How the Brain Works

Most of us know that we would not be much good without our brains, but we sometimes forget just how incredible that cerebral organ we carry around in our skull is.

From emotions to the choices and decisions we make, to our behavior and health, neuroscience shows us that the brain is the most amazing creation on Earth ... and the following are five reasons why:

### 1. It Keeps Us Toxin Free and Healthy

We know that all animal species need sleep, as much as they need food, water, and air. In humans, children need a lot of sleep to help them grow healthily.

But sleep is the occasion for another critical function in the adult brain—and it is not just a well-deserved rest from the stresses and strains of everyday life; it is a cleaning mechanism for the body.

A study published recently in the *Science* Journal shows that sleep ensures metabolic homeostasis. This means that it helps clean the brain; hidden "caves" in the brain are activated during sleep to bathe it in fluids and clear it from harmful toxins that can impact our daily performance and our overall health.

These toxins, which accumulate during waking hours, include proteins that have been linked with Alzheimer's disease.

### 2. Our Brains Make Us Social Creatures

Our brains thrive on being around others, and we really are social creatures. We are not alone in the animal kingdom in that respect, but partly what sets humans apart is the need to feel loved, to have friends, and to sympathize with others. Our brains are designed that way.

A study from the University of Virginia found that we associate those people who are closest to us, such as friends, spouses, and lovers, as part of ourselves. Other people become part of our own identity, and the feelings of love and empathy we have for them help to explain why it is so hard when these relationships break down; it also helps explain why when friends or loved ones are threatened, we feel threatened too.

Neuroscience suggests that humans have a physical and mental need to have friends and allies to identify and empathize with, in order to live a healthy life.

### 3. Your Brain is the Third Eye

A recent study published in the *Journal of Psychological Science* shows that the brain is able to process and understand visual input that our eyes do not pick up, and that we are not consciously aware of.

The study monitored brainwave patterns of subjects as they were shown a series of black silhouettes, some of which contained objects hidden in the white spaces on the outsides of the image.

They conclusively showed that the brain was able to process shapes and understand their meaning, even if the participant did not recognize consciously what they were.

### 4. Your Brain Has Amazing Powers of Communication

Did you know that your brain can send information directly to another brain?

In a pilot study, researchers at the University of Washington in Seattle investigated brain-to-brain communication. They designed a computer game-based task which two subjects could cooperatively solve by transmitting a meaningful signal from one brain to the other.

Using electroencephalography (EEG) to record brain signals and transcranial magnetic stimulation (TMS) for stimulating the brain, they found that information taken from one brain using EEG could be transmitted to another brain noninvasively using TMS. This potentially allows two people to cooperatively solve a task via direct brain-to-brain transfer of information.

### 5. Your Brain Fights Emotional Pain!

Humans have inbuilt responses to fighting pain, which can come in many forms—physical pain (which is in itself diverse) and emotional pain.

New research from a team at the University of Michigan shows that the brain is involved in controlling the effects of socially induced emotional pain—like when we are snubbed by friends or loved ones.

Using imaging techniques from neuroscience and an online dating model, it was found that the brain releases natural painkillers (opioids) to fight the pain of social rejection; these work to dampen the pain signals and originate from the same part of the brain that responds to physical pain.

# The Marvelous Growthof the Human Brain

What is it that makes us humans so special? Is there an area of the brain unique to humans? In the course of our colorful history, many attempts have been made to establish which particular features of the brain supplement you and me with our unique qualities.

It is tempting to guess that you simply have a bigger brain than other animals. But a small glimpse of the evidence quickly rules this possibility out; elephants have brain four times the size of our own, yet it is you that goes to the zoo and then checks out the elephants instead of the other way around.

The next step is to get a comparison of the relative size of brains among mammals, that is, the ratio of their brain mass to its body mass. But even in this category, small monkeys like the mouse lemur have outclassed us, humans, leaving us roughly against with bats and squirrels.

If you want some assurance of your special status as a human being, then it is found in the phenomenon of allometry, which indicates the expected brain size from an organism's body size. From this perspective, your brain is about five times larger than expected for a mammal of our size and about three times larger than expected for a primate of our size. So no need to worry that the squirrels in your backyard are organizing an attempt to attain total global domination; you are probably still quite a bit more capable than those little critters.

But where did your intelligence come from in the first place? Is there a particular reason for the fact that you are in possession of a fairly big brain? Quite a few interesting theories try to answer these questions, let us have a look at a few of the most interesting ones.

One of the theories states that your large brain is a product of the social world in which your ancestors evolved. Surely, all that chatting, deceiving, and partying with other cavemen required quite a bit of cognitive capacity and thus a larger brain.

The core of the theory is that primate intelligence allowed a caveman to serve his or her interest by interacting with others either in cooperation or manipulation but without disturbing the social balance of the group, something which increased his reproductive fitness and thus the spreading of his bigger brain genes.

This almost looks a bit like politics: the successful and cynical politician uses his position for his ends while appearing to serve the people, all without disrupting the elective system.

The increase in intelligence enjoyed by those socially active cavemen could then act as a positive feedback loop as competitors would gain the same increase in intelligence, thereby raising the level of intelligence to be reached for further advantages.

Quite a different theory simply suggests that the throwing of rocks must have stimulated your incredible brain growth. Imagine throwing a stone at a moving object, to hit it successfully requires the solution to a series of complex calculations and very fine motor tuning.

Variables that need to be factored into deciding the velocity, angle, and direction of aim include the mass and size of the stone, the direction of movement of the target, and the distance to the target. It almost sounds like rocket science, but still (most) humans are quite skilled in throwing things with some accuracy, at least, compared to other animals. Several researchers have suggested that the advantages to be gained from accurate throwing may have stimulated brain growth.

Another interesting theory also tries to explain the fact that your brain tripled in size in three million years, a very rapid process by evolutionary standards and something which left the other primates walking on all fours.

One force that has the potential to bring about such rapid change could be sexual selection.

It is suggested that humans would pick potential partners not only by observing their health, age, and fertility but also by their cognitive skills. Just like those beautiful peacocks displaying their tail to attract the opposite sex, males display their intellectual and cognitive skills through their complex storytelling and artful displays. These are something maintained in today's world as performances, for example, in art, science, and literature.

Presumably, females could be rather picky in choosing males, selecting those that were the most amusing, inventive, and had creative brains (among various other criteria).

Although increasing brain size was thus a process driven by female choice, fortunately, both sexes gradually increased their brain size, since large brains are needed to recognize and appreciate inventive male displays, which resulted in the equal distribution of intelligence observed in both men and women nowadays.

Now, besides the above theories, there are several other possible evolutionary stimuli which could have propelled the growth of the human brain. This including the demands of a varied diet as those cavemen enjoyed back in the old days, the advantages of language and the increase in brain size that this required, and the complex genetic processes related to genomic imprinting.

For all these explanations, there is, at least, some level of evidence to found which supports them. It is therefore probably a combination of different factors that has caused you to become so distinct from other life forms and gave rise to your great reasoning faculty.

How can you use this knowledge to enhance your brain? Well, for one thing, evolution acts over millions of years, making it rather hard to increase actively the size of your brain. But do not despair, as noted before, the brain is an incredibly flexible organ, which allows you to improve it in various ways.

One thing we have derived from this evolutionary analysis of brain growth is that social interaction has probably been rather important for your brain, and in order to maintain a healthy brain, you have to use it for which it was designed. In other words, make sure your life is not deprived of any social contacts, as your brain would not like it.

Now, how about throwing rocks? Well, I am not suggesting that everyone should practice rock throwing for hours per day to maintain healthy brains, but it is a fact that practicing some hand-eye coordinating activities increases your cognitive abilities and the number of synapses in the brain.

# Boost Your Brain Today

Increasing your mind capability requires steady effort over a period. In case you do, you may have to keep in mind that it cannot be attained overnight, but you can get fast results in case you work on it consistently.

You could essentially enhance your mind power ordinarily by using very simple procedures. In this book there are just a few of the procedures you can use to boost your intellect power:

*Attempt being two-handed*—Usually, people work with only one dominant hand. That is why individuals are identified as "left-handed" or "right-handed." That is done mostly out of convenience. People can, in fact, become ambidextrous. Both hands may be used for drawing, writing, etc. Attempt teaching yourself to become two-handed. You would be amazed how hard the brain will work to "teach" your other hand the tasks which were relegated to your dominant hand. Even you do not succeed instantly; the critical point is always that you are constantly endeavoring to learn something new.

*Challenge a number of your senses*—Usually, we come to depend on only on one or two senses (usually hearing and sight) but what can occur if you purposefully blocked out your significant senses?

The brain would have to work harder to compensate for your blocked senses. Blocking one or more of your senses is a nice brain exercise. You can try this easy brain-boosting exercise when doing simple routines such as walking and even when you are folding origami.

Just ensure that you are not driving a car or operating any machinery, then you could probably get yourself blindfolded or block out your own ears using earplugs without running into trouble. During the exercise, I would like you to immerse yourself in the experience of having to use your other senses to make sense of what is occurring. The more time you immerse yourself in this particular exercise, the higher the final results.

*Draw more frequently*—Drawing is simply one of many pleasurable methods you could express yourself. You do not have to be seriously fantastic at drawing; this is an exercise in getting better your brain ability, after all. Invest in a big drawing pad, so you can draw much more on a page. Draw when you feel satisfied, unfortunate, angry, or when you just feel like drawing. Use drawing like a vehicle to express your thoughts and emotions. Your brain will work not easily in expressing itself through lines and forms. Be much more creative and express yourself in several methods. The human brain has two primary divisions that represent two distinct thinking centers: the creative center and the logic center.

The logic center of the brain is commonly useful for trouble resolving and rationalizing while the creative center is used mainly for self-expression.

Most of the time, people overuse their logic centers while totally disregarding their creative sides. It is great in case you work in an environment that demands you to use your logic center much more (you are a computer programmer or mathematician); however, you still must balance your usage of both of those sides of the brain, so your brain power will not take a hit.

The easiest way to stimulate your creative center is by engaging in songs, art, and writing. There are a few actions needed to be sufficient for any person simply because when you start on only one of these actions, I am sure your days and nights will probably be filled with own pure satisfaction, and even more importantly, brain challenges inside the form discovering how to do things correct.

For example, if you prefer to understand ways to sketch realistic human figures, you have to find out how you can draw exact lines on paper. All of that effort challenges the brain, and the brain responds by increasing the amount of connections it has.

# The Five Natural Emotions

There are only five natural emotions we have, which we all experience. The other emotions are an offshoot of the five, and they come about when we manifest or express the five main ones.

How we express these can be good, and it can sometimes be negative.

The five natural emotions are grief, love, envy, anger, and fear.

In the following section, I will discuss each of these emotions and how we can express them in a good way to help us build and develop our character. I will also discuss how we can express them in a negative way which could be harmful and disadvantageous to the individual.

## Emotion of Grief

This is the emotion which connects us to the objects and people who are important to us. When we lose something or someone important through a natural or another form of separation, we experience a feeling of loss.

With the loss of a person through death, we become sad when we think about the reality of never seeing the person again.

So, we cry for the vacuum the person will leave in our lives. It is usually difficult to bear the feeling because there is nothing we can do to change it. Whether we like it or not, we have to accept the reality of their passing. The truth is we will never see the person or object again.

A lot of ways can be tried to be able to cope with our loss. One of which is talking about them. Those good and best moments we have shared with our loved ones can be recalled. Trying to express how we feel about that loss is another way of coping.

We can also convince ourselves that our loved ones are finally at rest, particularly if they had been sick and suffered for a very long period of time. Some deal with the situation by convincing themselves that the person they loved continues to live in an another life and are watching over them to ensure that they are alright.

Experiencing and going through a process of grief is important to us in many ways. First, it forces us to think about what we have lost and helps us accept the truth about what happened.

In this way, we can move on after a while, especially if we have dealt sufficiently with the feeling of loss.

Also, going through the grieving process help us to again be in touch with our godliness because we can feel and express the love and kindness in our hearts, which is important for us. Feeling and expressing these emotions reminds us of our goodness and closeness to the Almighty.

Sometimes we struggle to overcome the feeling, and it stays with us for an extended period. The reason we struggle is we cannot accept that the person has left us. We cannot see a way to be happy without them.

This is a normal process of healing. Everybody experiences it to a lesser or greater extent, depending on their strength, and how close they were to the departed person.

Staying with the feeling for a long period has several disadvantages.

One is we will not have the strength to focus on the important tasks. If we do not focus, we will not do what we need to do to achieve our goals. Also, the quality of our lives will be negatively affected.

## Emotion of Love

Love is the feeling we have when we appreciate something. Many people consider living a godly emotion because it represents goodness and is the basis of everything is good.

Love allows us to understand and to accept everything for what it is without passing judgment.

Love creates a strong bond between people. When there is love, people feel safe to be authentic without fear of recrimination or hurt because they know they are in good company.

We express love with kindness, respect, sincerity, prayer, and others. Personal values like kindness, sincerity, respect, and so on are based on love.

The opposite of love is hate. Where there is hatred, there is hurt, pain, jealousy, and unhappiness.

We need to express this emotion always to build healthy, positive relationships with people. Without it, it is not possible to have positive and meaningful relations with others.

Expressing this emotion is the highest form of development and indicates the maturity of the soul because it suggests an advanced understanding of life and nature.

## Emotion of Envy

Envy is when we acknowledge others and what they have or has achieved. The acknowledgment could be of their material possessions or other forms of achievement.

When expressed in love and sincerity, it is a compliment to the other person as it acknowledges them and expresses a recognition of what they have.

All people have this feeling at one or other time. It is a good emotion because it is a way we show our natural longing for growth. This is because it allows us to want better and bigger things for ourselves. Without the feeling, we would not have the need or desire to progress or improve.

When we lose control of our minds by not focusing on expressing the emotion positively, we become jealous of others. We start to think we are more deserving than they are.

## Emotion of Anger

This is the feeling we get when things go against what we expect or want them to. Usually, we get the feeling when we are struggling to accept what happened. Mostly, it is when we think we or someone else could have done something differently to prevent the situation we are in from happening.

The feeling of anger manifests in several ways. However, the message we send by expressing the feeling is that of disappointment and sometimes hurt.

This is an ordinary feeling, and we all get it from time to time.

Anger is important in that it helps us to identify instances that are not in line with what we know and believe or agree.

A positive use of the feeling helps us build relationships that are based on trust and honesty because we can tell others how we feel about what they had done. This will help them understand us better, which is an important requirement for building positive relationships.

Uncontrolled anger can become manic and sometimes violent, which can lead to negative results, not conducive to a relationship building environment.

If negative, anger can become self-centered and lead us to want things to go our way and to hurt others.

## Emotion of Fear

Fear is a feeling of anxiety of apprehension we get when we are uncertain of the outcomes. Often, we feel it when we are afraid the outcomes might be something bad for us.

The feeling manifests in many ways, and the way it does depends on its severity and on a person's ability to deal with it.

In its mildest form, fear can manifest in anxiety which may be overcome through the power of will. However, in other cases, it can become so overwhelming that a person is not able to focus and to do their normal tasks.

We all have and will always encounter in our lives the emotion called Fear. Both positive and negative manners are manifested, the same as the others.

Fear helps us in focusing and producing our best efforts when we express it positively; if we are afraid of it, we might fail. It helps us muster the confidence and strength we needed to get through something challenging in our lives. It does this by helping us to recognize the threat and seriousness of the situation, thus motivating us to do what is important and necessary to get the results we want.

In its negative form, it can become a panic attack, distress, dread, or horror.

Depending on its severity and our ability to control it, fear can immobilize us and prevent us from operating normally. This may affect our ability to perform normally and to produce our best efforts in the things we do.

When it is uncontrolled, fear manifests in behaviors such as avoidance of certain situations. These are usually seen as threatening in some way, and therefore not good for the person. Most importantly, the result of uncontrolled fear is that it reduces a person's effectiveness in what they do.

We are all born with these emotions. Our task and responsibility are to use them to help us grow and be mature. We cannot do anything to avoid them. These emotions are part of our natural endowment. We have to live with them, one way or another.

These emotions can be allowed to overcome us, to control us, and to determine how we live and the quality of our lives, depending on us. Or we can use them positively to help us develop our personality and character.

Accepting these emotions as part of our life is the way to do this because they are the means by which we can get to experience who we truly are and the life we are living.

We can experience all the other emotions only through them. We cannot talk about achieving happiness when we are still in their clutches and under their control.

It is not possible to have contentment when we are still fighting to master them. It is impossible to feel kindness when we are still struggling to love.

We cannot care for the good of others when we do not conquer selfishness and jealousy.

Many of what we want will depend on us in dealing with these emotions on our terms. Failing to deal with them will mean we allow ourselves to be controlled by them. When this happens, we will only express their extreme counterpart, which can be to our disadvantage and detriment.

Many of what we want will also depend on us in refusing to be held as a hostage by our own grief for having lost something that is valuable.

They depend on how we can move on despite what we have been through.

They depend on us being able to overcome our insecurities, which can prevent us from pursuing our goals by doing what is necessary to reach them.

They depend on us being able to realize that we must keep a cool head in all situations if we want to be effective in all matters of our life.

They depend on us being able to rejoice at other people successes and achievements, instead of wanting to compete with them or to bring them down.

So, in all matters, we need to make sure that we have full control of our thoughts and emotions, so we can express or manifest only the positive sides of the five natural emotions. In this way, not only we will benefit by producing positive outcomes but also we will espouse the natural goodness we have.

The pain we experience through our emotional senses serves to help us grow and mature. It is the only way nature has provided for us to learn and develop our highest capabilities, which are to have full control of our thoughts and feelings.

The author is a human development specialist. His main interest is in helping people learn the skills to live a happy and successful lives. He does this by teaching them to set goals and providing them with strategies which they can apply to reach them.

He believes that it is important to know and understand the laws of nature, so one can use them to their benefit by working with them, instead of against them.

His other interests are in finding more creative ways to help people achieve the success they want and to be happy.

In addition to personal development and growth, he is involved in running a consultancy business that gives a wide range of services geared toward helping other companies benefit from the functions of their human resources.

# Worry and Stress and How They Affect Us

Perhaps you have heard the story of Chicken Little. Chicken Little was in the woods one day when an acorn fell on her head. She became scared and thought that the sky was falling. She resolved that she had to tell the king about this great disaster. While on her way, she meets Henny Penny. She tells him of her experience. He joins her in going to the king. Eventually, others join her including Ducky Lucky, Goosey Loosey, and Turkey Lurkey. Finally, they encounter Foxy Loxy and tell him about the problem. He replies that he will show them the way to the king but instead leads them straight to his den. Chicken Little and her companions never saw the king to tell him that the sky is falling. Stress, worry, and fear are killers.

## Stress

Genesis 21: 8–21 gives us the story of Hagar and her son Ishmael. Hagar was a servant of Abraham and Sarah. When Sarah could not conceive, she gave Hagar to Abraham so that he could sleep with her. This was a normal custom in Abraham's day to ensure that a person had a descendant. Hagar conceived, and Ishmael was born. However, Sarah eventually conceived a son. When Sarah saw Ishmael mocking her son Isaac, she demanded that Abraham sends Hagar and her son away. Abraham complied. While in the desert, Hagar exhausted all of the provisions and feared that she and her son would die. God, however, came to her rescue. Hagar faced a stressful situation but was delivered through God's grace.

Stress can be defined as a struggle that causes worry or emotional tension. While various situations are potential stressors, ultimately stress has to do with how we respond to the situations of life. In other words, what causes me stress may not cause you stress because of how you choose to deal with it. There are numerous results of stress. Persons who are stressed out have difficulty remembering things; they lack the ability to concentrate, and they often exercise poor judgment (they tend to react rather than to respond to situations). They also see only the negative, are anxious, or have racing thoughts, and are constantly worrying. They experience moodiness, irritability or short temper, agitation, and are unable to relax. They tend to feel overwhelmed, have a sense of loneliness and isolation, and to feel depressed or unhappy.

## Anxiety

Anxiety can be described as an inner feeling of apprehension, uneasiness, concern, worry, and fear; the body is ready to flee or fight. The Bible has numerous verses on anxiety and fear. In the New Testament, the word for anxiety is used in two ways. It is used to speak of a healthy concern (2 Corinthians 11: 28; Philippians 2: 20). This is something positive: we are expected to be concerned about our family, our church, our society, and other persons and things in life. This is a natural outworking of our love for God and others. Anxiety also refers to fret or worry (Psalms 94: 19; Matthew 6: 25–34; Philippians 4: 6, 7; 1 Peter 5: 7); this is its negative use. It is a failure to trust God, and a belief that we alone are responsible for handling problems. We begin to see things from a strictly natural perspective rather than from God's perspective. It is wrong and unhealthy to be paralyzed by worry.

There can be various causes of anxiety. We become anxious when there is a threat to something that we consider to be important. The danger is a threat; this includes such things as crime, violent weather, and unexplained or unexpected illness. This anxiety comes because the person is uncertain about what to expect and feels helpless to prevent or reduce the threat. We also become anxious whenever our self-esteem is threatened. People like to look good and perform well, so they are bothered when other people make them look bad. They are also bothered when there is anything that affects their ability to execute any task. Some people may be afraid of new social situations because they do not know how to react or how others will perceive them.

Another threat that produces anxiety is separation. We become anxious when we are separated from significant others. For example, separation and/

or divorce can result in anxiety. The death of a loved one also leads to anxiety. Anxiety is also produced when our values are threatened. For example, the child who turns away from the family beliefs may cause anxiety for his parents. In the church, we may become anxious because a ministry head or pastor may want to change tradition and institute something new. We can also include under threats unconscious influences. These are potential stresses that people tend to ignore. However, unresolved issues will accumulate and cause anxiety to build up.

People become anxious whenever they are faced with a conflict; persons are faced with two or more pressures and must decide what to do. They may choose to either avoid the conflict or deal with it. For example, after an intense quarrel, a husband may choose to avoid conflict by not talking to his wife, or he can choose to deal with the conflict by talking with her in the attempt to resolve the problem. There are some conflicts we may both avoid and deal with. This seems somewhat contradictory. This simply is the fork in the road where we have to choose one option over another. Sometimes it may be a matter of choosing the lesser of two evils.

People often have irrational beliefs that result in fear. Someone has developed an acrostic for fear—false expectation appearing real. People are afraid of many things. They are afraid of intimacy—of getting too close to others. They are afraid of being known: would people accept them if they knew them? Some persons are afraid of rejection; perhaps they were rejected in the past by a significant other or someone that they cared about. Others are afraid of acting inappropriately, especially in a new setting. People have a fear of being hurt (emotionally or physically). Other fears include fear of people, taking risks, the unknown, losing a job, not being able to find a job, losing a spouse, and losing a child. Other fears are the following: losing health, not having enough, of aging, of injury, of death, of being able to perform sexually, of children leaving home, of taking an exam, or doing a course of study. The reality is that fear affects all categories of our lives: spiritual, emotional, mental, physical, financial, vocational, family, and societal.

People become anxious when they have unmet needs. Abraham Maslow was an American psychologist who is famous for developing a hierarchy of needs. He identified these as falling into the following categories typically in ascending order: physiological, security, love and belonging, esteem, and self-actualization. Failure to have any of these needs met can result in anxiety. For example, we may become anxious if a storm blows the roof off of our house exposing us to the elements. This is a physiological need, and we may be worried about where we are going to stay, particularly if we do not have any family nearby or any close friends to turn to. Here is another example: a woman wants to feel loved by her husband and becomes anxious when she finds that he is not spending quality time with her and that he is distant and aloof. Her need for security, love, and belonging is not being met, which produces anxiety.

Physical disorders can bring anxiety and panic-like symptoms; medical treatment, therefore, is necessary. There are other things that can lead to anxiety. People can learn to be anxious from the teaching and examples of others. Anxious parents typically will produce anxious children; children learn to be afraid of people and various situations. Some people because of their personality are more prone to be anxious than others, particularly persons who tend to be meticulous and highly introspective. Social environment can also play a factor; for example, negative economic trends and change moral standards can lead to anxiety. Recession can translate into lower wages, loss of job, family stress, lifestyle changes, depletion of savings, increasing debt, loss of insurances and pensions, and the sacrifice of children's education. What we believe also determines our level of anxiety: do we have faith that God is loving, sovereign and omnipotent, or have we made Him too small in our eyes?

Anxiety can affect us in different ways. There can be physical reactions: anxiety can result in ulcers, headaches, skin rashes, shortness of breath, loss of appetite, and other physical ailments. If these problems persist over time, they cause the body to break down. There are also psychological reactions. Anxiety reduces productivity, hinders interpersonal relationships, stifles creativity and originality, dulls the personality, and affects the ability to think and remember. There can be defensive reactions such as ignoring the feelings of anxiety, pretending the situation that is causing the anxiety does not exist, blaming someone else for one's problems and slipping into childish ways of behavior. Defensive reactions include escapism through media such as drugs, alcoholism, pornography, and shopping. Another defensive reaction is focusing on other people's problems, trying to save other people without first looking to secure and save yourself. There can be positive or negative spiritual reactions to anxiety. Some people turn to God when they are anxious, depending on Him to see them through their difficulties. Others turn away from God—not praying, not reading Scripture, not going to church, and becoming bitter or angry with God.

The Scriptures give us an antidote for dealing with worry, fear, and stress in Philippians 4: 4–9. We are told to rejoice in the Lord. Nothing beats thanksgiving, praise, worship, and rejoicing in taking our minds off of ourselves and our situations and putting our minds firmly on God, His power, love, grace, wisdom, and mercy. We are also admonished to be gentle with others. People who are harsh, critical, and judgmental will be anxious people and are always concerned about whether the people around them are meeting their standards. Gentleness allows us to be patient with and empathetic toward others. Worship and prayer are inextricably connected: either prayer leads to worship or worship leads to prayer. We must learn to commit every situation to God in prayer, releasing our faith to believe God to intervene in our problems or to give us His grace to endure. Our thinking also has to change; this is where we need God to renew our minds and help us to meditate on those things that are positive, noble, and of good report. Negativity will always cause us anxiety. We can focus on the problems around us or the positive promises of God. Another Scriptural principle is to be obedient by putting into practice what the Word of God teaches us.

Anxiety often comes because people lack self-confidence. God has given us certain inert abilities to deal with the stressors of life. Persons who lack self-confidence do not trust themselves to handle those stressors. The lack of self-confidence also translates into a lack of faith. Such persons need to develop self-confidence: a belief in their abilities to meet the challenges and dangers of life. Worry can be alleviated by getting involved in work and other activities. This expands nervous energy and distracts from the anxiety-producing situation. Passivity and inactivity will cause us to focus on our worries. We should also have faith in the ability and confidence of leaders who can deal with anxiety. There are times that the situation is so overwhelming that we need to turn to others for help. So there is nothing to get embarrassed about this situation as God has made us interdependent and interlinked with other believers.

We must learn to cope by admitting fears and anxieties when they arise, talking these over with other people, building and maintaining relationships, and learning principles and techniques of relaxation. People who tend to worry a lot can be workaholics who take no time to rest. Every Christian needs to schedule a day of rest, recreation, and relaxation. God modeled this when He determined that we should work for six days then rest on the seventh. The Sabbath does not have to be legalistically observed on the seventh day, but it should be incorporated into our weekly schedule. It is also necessary to evaluate our priorities, goals, and use of time. This has to do with our Christian stewardship. Those persons who are focused merely on success and worldly pursuits will find much to worry about. The Bible clearly shows that our priority must be in God's kingdom and His righteousness. We are in transit, and all of our life choices must be to glorify God. Managing our time carefully eliminates stress because we adequately set aside time for all the major things we have to do.

It is imperative that we keep things in perspective: do not assume that the worse will happen in different situations. The Bible encourages us to have hope, which is the confident expectation of something good. We need to know that "all things God works for the good of those who love him, who have been called according to His purpose" (Romans 8: 28). We also need to reach out to others. People who are self-centered are always plagued with anxiety. There is something therapeutic about helping others. Scripture tells us that it is more blessed to give than to receive. Jesus modeled this and said that He came to serve. We release the blessings of God including peace by blessing others. The most important principle in preventing anxiety is to have faith in God. We must learn to trust God regardless of the situation. We must trust in the sovereignty of God and trust in His ability to powerfully intervene in the situations of our lives. People who are continually anxious are not people of faith. They magnify their problems rather than put faith in God.

Let those words, as well as these following Scriptures, encourage you: The LORD bless you and keep you; the LORD make His face shine upon you and be gracious to you; the LORD turn His face toward you and give you peace. Numbers 6: 24–26.

For to us a child is born, to us, a son is given, and the government will be on his shoulders. And he will be called Wonderful Counselor, Mighty God, Everlasting Father, Prince of peace. Isaiah 9: 6.

Peace I leave with you; my peace I give you. Do not let your hearts be troubled and do not be afraid. John 14: 27.

You will keep in perfect peace those whose minds are steadfast because they trust in you. Isaiah 26: 3.

# Learning How to Control Your Emotions

Do you feel like you cannot seem to control your emotions? Maybe you lash out at others around you and later feel bad about it. If you are like me, you think that something is wrong with you because you just cannot seem to control your emotions. One day I would wake up crying feeling all emotional and then the next day I am happy as to be. I use to think that I was bipolar or something because of how my emotions would shift from time to time. I would lash out at whoever was around me and would not think twice about it. There was a time in my life when others thought I was unable to feel emotions because I acted as if I did not care about nothing, and nothing seem to affect me. Why is that? Why do some people feel and think like they cannot control their emotions? Why do others act as if they are unable to feel anything at all?

A number of people allow their own emotions to control them and their lives. They allow their emotions to dictate how they are going to feel this day. They allow their emotions to tell them how to act when someone make them mad. Let us take anger as an example. You may be struggling with anger issues, and you constantly feel like that there is something wrong with you for feeling anger all of the time. Anger is just an emotion. Anger is placed inside of us to help us know when someone is taking advantage of us and when something is not right. We are not to act on anger, but it is normal to feel anger. God wants us to learn how to control our anger. The Bible says "In your anger, do not sin." God does not want you to walk around always mad about something. He wants you to get to the root of what is causing you so much anger in the first place.

Have you ever encountered an emotionless person? They seem like they do not feel anything inside. They tend to hide their emotions from others and even their relatives to see. People who have been so bruised and hurt so badly in their past experiences easily put up their own walls around them and adopt this emotionless demeanor by themselves. They can also feel pain just like we do; they are just unable to express and show them to others. I was this type of person, and I have notice how some of my friends would say stuff like, "what's wrong with you. You act like you don't even care about nothing." That was my way of not allowing myself to get hurt again. I train myself to respond that way toward people. I still felt pain inside. I just did not show them my pain.

So how can you start to control your emotions and not let your emotions control you?

- Shift your emotions to feel happier when you wake up early in the morning and find yourself feeling down, depressed, or just sad about yourself. How do you shift your emotions? The way how I shift my emotions to feel much happier is by listening to music. I listen to music that is going to lift me up. I also start dancing as I am listening to my music. It is hard to feel sad about yourself if you are up singing and dancing to some good music.

- Fight against your emotions. Be still and quiet for a minute, and just listen to what is going on inside of you. Whatever your mad at may not even be the real problem. You may just need some sleep, so instead of venting out your emotions, get silence and figure out what has got you upset.

- Pray about your emotions. Ask God to help you deal with controlling your anger, mouth, and emotions. Whatever area you are struggling in, give it to God to take care of it for you. Now when you give it to God, God may not simply take away your anger. He may start showing you exactly why back in your past the reason you may be angry in the first place. God will show you the root first before He takes away the problem you are having. You have to be open to receive what He shows you and tells you, so you can get healed from your past and start moving past your anger.

You can control your emotions. You have the power over your emotions. Start today controlling them and not allowing them to control you. If you enjoyed this amazing book, then share your thoughts with me below by leaving me a comment. Please also share this with others. Go ahead and subscribe here so that you can receive your free entrepreneur road map guide filled with powerful dynamic information that I know that it will take your life to the next level. I look forward to hearing from you.

# Thoughts and Emotions in Our Spiritual Journey

Many people wonder why people go through difficult and challenging experiences.

They wonder why most of what we learn are in life is through the hard way. Why we learn the most valuable life lessons through pain and emotional hurt. They wonder if it is a fate which causes them to go through these, or is it because of their actions.

Is it the law of action-reaction at play?

People go through all these, sometimes, without anything which suggests that they played a part in causing them. These events and occurrences happen nevertheless.

Is life designed in that way? For us to learn through pain?

It appears we feel more human and spiritually connected when we are going through difficult times than when all is going well for us.

There is a sense that when we are going through trials and troubles, we are more humble and kind than when all is well.

If kindness, goodness, and humility are the emotions we must express, then why could not we just be humble and kind all the time so that we could be spared from emotional hurt and other challenges.

All these questions are answered here.

Thoughts and Emotions

Nature gives us opportunities to develop those areas of our personality and character which need development. By developing these, we learn to control all areas of our lives and achieve happiness and fulfillment.

All the experiences we go through serve to develop those specific areas.

Our emotions are what make us who we are. They also connect us to the source or our true nature.

Emotions do not have thought, reasoning, or logical component. They always manifest in their crude and pure form.

That is why we must use our thinking to control them so that they do not get out of hand.

Part of our purpose and responsibility in life is to learn to master ourselves. This means we must learn to control our thoughts. If we can control our thoughts, we will be able to control our emotions.

Our thoughts are the only tool we have to control our emotions or how we feel.

We go through various conditions and circumstances to develop this ability—to control our thoughts so that we can control our emotions.

So when we know the emotions which keep us grounded, and in touch with the source, we will try to stay with those emotions. We will try to learn to control our minds, so we will stay with the emotions.

In time, we will realize the only way to be happy is to control our minds. In this way, we can freely choose how we want to think and feel, under any conditions and circumstances.

It does not mean that to be in touch with the source we must expose ourselves to hurtful conditions. This is not necessary because it is nature's duty to do that, and it does it well.

The conditions we go through help us see the full picture. They serve to help us see the other side, so we will know both sides.

When we know both sides and can accept and live with both, we will reach the stage of development and growth we need to be fully mature.

Our greatest challenge and difficulty right now is to accept these two at the same time. We have conditioned ourselves to be happy only when conditions are favorable, and everything is going well for us. So we want to keep this for as long as possible.

In our effort to do that, we forget the other side exists. When nature shakes us into awareness of the opposite conditions, we wonder why. This is because we have not accepted that the other side is also part of the experience we need.

Staying for too long in a blissful state or experience can make us complacent, and we forget to express the qualities which help us become better people. It can alienate us from the feelings of love and kindness, which are the characteristics of a grounded feeling.

We have tendencies to focus on enjoying the joy and glamor of our lives, and the vices that come with it, when the things in our lives are going well for us. We tend to forget the need to be humble and to express goodness and virtue to others.

We use the senses nature gave us to experience life.

In addition to taste, smell, touch, and sight, we use our emotions to experience life and to learn important lessons about ourselves. The lessons we get from our emotions are profound and contribute significantly to developing our souls and character.

# Biblical Perspective—Forgiveness is an Important Key to Emotional Healing

T ext: Matthew 6: 12, 14–15; Matthew 18: 21–35

This goes without any question that there are a lot of people who are hurting in our society. These people feel both emotionally damaged and dysfunctional in their work. We all go through various situations that we feel will overwhelm us at some point in our life chapters. These situations leave us feeling angry, discouraged, disappointed, and depressed, as well as frustrated. We may want to react by lashing out, withdrawing, giving up, or ending it all. We are human beings, and we hurt, at times intensely. Broken items can be repaired, and God can heal hurting persons. One important key to being healed is forgiveness.

## The Prayer and the Parable

There are several things that we can look at in the prayer that Jesus taught us and the parable He shared with the disciples on forgiveness. We are only entitled to pray for forgiveness if we have already forgiven others. To forgive is to let go, to give up debt by not demanding it. Debt is literally that which is owed, but in this context, it refers to sin. People will sin against us, and the principle is simple: if we forgive them, God will forgive us. The rabbis of the day recommended forgiving no more than three times. Peter, therefore, was being Peter being generous by mentioning seven times. Jesus' response would have been a shock to the disciples and would have gone against all that they had been taught. Forgiveness was not to be at a mere seven times but was to be done seventy times seven, a number that refers to the unlimited amount (the multiples of seven signify perfection).

Jesus tells us a parable about an unmerciful servant to illustrate His point. This servant owed his master with 10,000 talents. At that time, a talent was the highest unit of currency, and each talent was equivalent to 15 years of wages. Jesus made this story of the servant even more dramatic by using the number "10,000," which was the highest Greek numeral. This would mean that the servant owed 150,000 years of wages. The king threatened punishment against the man and his family: They would be sold into slavery to repay the debt. The servant begged and promised to pay back everything. This was, of course, impossible and may indicate the kind of dishonest character of the servant. The master was gracious and canceled the debt.

We go from one scene to another scene. The servant went out and found one of his fellow servants who only owed him a small amount: A denarius was only worth one day's wage, so the second servant only owed 100-day wages. The servant to whom the debt was owed grabbed the man and began to choke him and demanded that the man pays back all he owed. That man essentially used the same words that the servant had used—"be patient with me." However, the first servant refused and had the man thrown into prison.

Let us go to the final scene. Some other servants of the King reported the matter to their master who called in the previously forgiven servant. He labeled the servant wicked and turned him over to the jailers to be tortured. The torturers are those persons who elicit the pain and truth by the use of the rack. Jesus wraps up the parable with a sobering statement, "This is how my Heavenly Father will treat each of you unless you forgive your brother from your heart" (meaning forgive your brother sincerely).

## The Debts Owed to Us

People can do a lot to us whether deliberately or unintentionally. Persons have been the victim of various forms of abuse: physical, sexual, emotional, verbal, neglect, and spiritual. Spiritual abuse is a form of emotional abuse where Christians control and manipulate other believers. Often it is identified with pastors/priests who abuse their authority. It can incorporate the other forms of abuse. This particular abuse is extremely damaging because we expect a higher standard from ministers of the gospel. We expect them to be the men and women of integrity. They represent the Lord Jesus Christ.

Some people will gossip about us; sometimes the more successful and progressive you are, the more people find something to say about you. Other individuals will blatantly lie about or to us. Some Christians have been the victims of unfaithfulness. Their spouse may have been cheating on them for years and to rub salt into the wounds, they may have been doing so indiscriminately and unapologetically. Things like that can leave a spouse devastated.

Some persons have been the victims of assault. Some children have been or are being bullied at school. Others know what it is to be attacked, beaten, and robbed. They may know what it is for someone to break into their homes. There are those who have experienced the horrors of rape, their bodies violated, in some cases, by a person that was trusted. Some have been the victims of accidents, or their loved one was injured or killed because of the recklessness of someone else. Some of us know what it is to be subject to control and manipulation: this could be an employer, a pastor, a family member, and a friend. It may have been that at the time we were naïve or immature and did not quite understand well that we were being taken advantage of.

We may also experience someone hurting or killing a friend, family member, or even someone that we respect. This can result in strong feelings of rage and desire for retaliation, even though we were not the victims. We can be offended by others in a number of different ways. For example, somebody fails to speak to you, your spouse fails to compliment you, someone may accidentally step on your foot, you did not receive what you wanted for your birthday. These things may seem slight, but we can be offended by them. All of the above are "debts" that people owe us, sins that they have perpetrated against us. There may be the feeling, therefore, that we have a right to hold on to these things.

## The Damage of Unforgiveness

Unforgiveness can lead to hatred, which can start with strong feelings of dislike. Based on what the person has done to you, you determine that you do not like him or her. You reach a place where you do not want to see that person. This can degenerate into wishing that something bad would happen to the person. You may even pray imprecatory prayers over the person, for example, praying that God will kill them or cause them to get into an accident; instead of adopting a position of blessing, you adopt a position of cursing. You may also try to undermine the person through such things as gossip, slander, and passive aggression.

*Unforgiveness leads to anger.* Persons are angry at those who have hurt them, not a passing anger (that is normal when a person has been hurt), but an abiding anger, anger that is settled and becomes the dominant emotion. Persons who are angry ruminate on the injury that was done to them; that is, their mind recycles the hurt—they constantly rehearse what the person did to them. This intensifies the anger. Holding on to anger can also lead to displaced aggression, in which persons take out their anger on the innocent, sometimes, in addition to retaliating against the person who had hurt them. In some cases, hurt and angry persons may not have the capacity or the opportunity to take out their anger on the person responsible for their hurt, so they turn to a substitute. While anger that is externalized leads to aggression, anger that is internalized leads to depression. Persons who are unable or unwilling to act on their anger become depressed.

*Unforgiveness also leads to bitterness.* Defining bitterness is hard. It is a combination of intense anger, feelings of disappointment, vindictiveness, hatred, negativity, and feelings of not getting what you deserved or that you have been ill-treated. People who harbor unforgiveness internalize anger to the point that they become bitter. Bitter people are always critical, spiteful (desire to take revenge, to lash out), and have a victim mentality (they feel that life and people are against them).

The most critical effect of unforgiveness is spiritual separation. Unforgiveness and all of its negative emotions affect our relationship with God. Unforgiveness affects our ability to pray, worship, apply the Word, and enjoy loving fellowship with the saints. The efficacy of our prayers is hindered, and we also do not usually feel like praying when we have unforgiveness in our hearts. The same applies to our worship and the reading and application of the Word. Unforgiveness hinders our ability to both love and is loved, leading to fractured relationships in the church. Unless unforgiveness is repented of it will destroy our relationship with God. It can also lead to spiritual deception: you are holding persons in your heart, but you believe that God is answering your prayers. You believe that God is enjoying your worship. You believe that you have an intimate relationship with God. This is serious spiritual deception; love for God must be vitally connected with love for the people around us.

Holding on to unforgiveness can cause disorientation: you do not feel like yourself. To use a cliché, you do not know if you are going or coming. You are being controlled by the person that you are holding in your heart. Sometimes, those individuals may not even be aware that they have caused offense, or they may not be thinking of the pain and the hurt they caused. The devil is also influencing you. Unforgiveness can also lead to mental illness. It can result in neurosis—mental and emotional problems. You begin to live in a fantasy world, a world of lies and deception to cover up the pain that you are feeling. Defense mechanisms kick in, and you retreat into a bubble to protect yourself.

Some people who have unforgiveness in their heart experience physical sickness. While joy and peace have positive effects on the body, unforgiveness has a detrimental effect on the body. Both experience and studies indicate that negative emotions can result in various sicknesses. Unforgiveness blocks your prayers, so it becomes a barrier to healing. Some persons wanted to be healed, and nothing happened until they forgave a person that they were angry with. The man is the body, soul, and spirit: whatever affects the body can affect the soul and the spirit; whatever affects the soul can affect the body and the spirit.

It is no surprise that unforgiveness leads to broken relationships. It has destroyed numerous marriages. Husbands or wives could not let go of some issue; anger and bitterness resulted leading to separation and eventually divorce. Forgiveness potentially leads to reconciliation. If couples practice forgiveness, then they will be able to maintain a good marriage; conflicts that could have destroyed the marriage are dealt with. Broken relationships are not limited to the home. Friendships and work relationships can be destroyed. Relationships in the church can also be destroyed: pastors and congregants can be alienated; members can be hostile to each other, and unfortunately, pastors could be unforgiving to other pastors.

Earlier, I mentioned not feeling like yourself because of the influence of the devil. Unforgiveness can eventually lead to demonic oppression and in extreme cases to possession. Unforgiveness displaces God and opens you to the influence of demonic spirits. It allows demonic strongholds to develop in your life. Unforgiveness can also affect work performance. You can become so angry and bitter that you do not properly focus on your work, work quality diminishes, and relationships are negatively affected. Unforgiveness leads to self-defeating and destructive behavior. It causes you to do foolish things: react with bad attitudes, do things to get back at people; it prevents you from getting ahead, being focused and taking good care of yourself (physically, spiritually, and emotionally).

## Learning to Let Go

Life can be antagonistic, and we will get hurt to lesser or greater degrees. Processing your hurt is important. This involves admitting it and thinking it through. You are not obsessively dwelling on the hurt, but you are processing what happened and how you feel about it. Are you disappointed, angry, or hurt? Did you do anything wrong that justified the person's action or reaction? Is there a reason a person may have done a particular thing? Processing the hurt means that you do not deny what has happened. Some people brush off incidents; they refuse to deal with any difficult situations in their lives. However, such denial leads to suppression, which leads to spiritual, emotional, and physical problems.

While we need to forgive others, we also need to ask for forgiveness from God and others. We need forgiveness for harboring negative emotions, for reacting wrongly to hurt, and for holding on to the hurt. We need to recognize that God had forgiven us (when we accepted Jesus Christ as our personal Lord and Savior), He forgives us now (when we confess and repent of our sins), and He will continue to forgive us (because of His grace and faithfulness). The debt we owed Him was greater than anything anyone owes us. Remember the example of Jesus: He was mocked, His beard was pulled out, He was beaten, stripped naked, and crucified on a cross, yet He forgave.

Ask God to fill you with His love and the other fruit of the Holy Spirit. Galatians 5: 22, 23 lists the fruit of the Spirit as "love, joy, peace, patience, kindness, goodness, faithfulness, gentleness, and self-control." Out of these aforementioned qualities, the most important is love which is deep, unconditional, and has a positive regard for others. It is based not only on what people can do but also on what God has done for us. We have to love all people even those who have hurt us especially our enemies. To love others in this way can only be done through the indwelling of the Holy Spirit. In other words, love is a supernatural trait that comes from God. God demonstrated this kind of love when He sent His Son Jesus Christ to die for the penalty of man's sin.

An important part of forgiveness is learning to forgive yourself. Sometimes we have a hard time forgiving ourselves, and therefore, we find it hard to forgive others. We may tend to condemn ourselves, which leads to feelings of guilt, anxiety, frustration, discouragement, and depression. The Bible makes it clear that there is no condemnation for the person who is in Christ Jesus (Romans 8: 1). If we have confessed our sins, then God applies His grace, love, blood, and forgiveness. Therefore, we have no right to continue to condemn ourselves. The devil is the one who accuses us, and we are not to partner with him and take ownership of his accusations. Tell yourself, "I am forgiven and I forgive myself."

In order to forgive those who have extensively hurt us, we must need to make the effort to understand these kinds of people. We need to study and learn as much as we can and know about human nature, the differences between them and us, the things that "make us tick" or trigger our emotions, and their background which are experiences that have shaped these kinds of people). Through these information, we will have realistic expectations of these people and to understand them fully and why people may react the way that they do. These is in no way excuses what people do, but it does allow us to empathize, know, and find it in our hearts to forgive them and to even reach out to help the person who has hurt us.

We must learn to talk to others. There is a misconception that we must be able to handle all issues on our own. In Galatians 6, two burdens are mentioned. One is the burden that each must carry—this is his/her share of the load. There is another burden that must be shared—this burden is too heavy for one person to carry. God has put us in a body of believers for a reason. The church has its flaws, but there are loving persons that we can talk to that can help us through difficult situations. Learn to talk to a trusted friend or a minister of the gospel. They can pray with and for you, listen empathetically, and provide guidance that can help you to release those hurts that persons have caused you.

God's grace is greater than any hurt. Regardless of what persons have done to you, God can give you the ability and the capacity to overcome. He has called you to live a life of victory. When you learn to forgive and when you let go, it will bring freedom, deliverance, and blessings.

# The Emotionally Healing Benefits From Sincere Praise and Worship are Immense

Turn with me to these concluding verses in this amazing letter to the Hebrews. I have been studying it recently and find it a rich vein of Scripture and so highly relevant and practical for the days in which we are living. These believers in Jesus Christ were being encouraged to submit to their leaders, to those who were over them.

It is not enough just to look to Jesus but also to those to whom Jesus has delegated authority. This can have problems, and this can be misused and abused.

Leaders have to remember that they are held responsible to Almighty God. All of us one day will have to give an account.

Sheep will be better disciples when submitting to shepherds. The leader has been thrust into this and keeps watch.

When a sheep gets into trouble, that causes the shepherd to be sad. Make their work a joy, not a burden. That is what the writer is encouraging these disciples of Jesus Christ to do. These leaders in the early Church experienced joy and grief.

They were also being asked to offer a sacrifice of praise. Praise is so vitally important. There are many people who never really praise Almighty God and give thanks to Jesus Christ.

As you praise, you find burdens becoming lighter and frustrations evaporating.

Any sense of guilt can disappear as we come before Almighty God in the name of Jesus Christ and praise His Holy Name. When we praise God, we become less critical and less judgmental. That must be a good thing.

When we praise God, we will stop complaining about our hurts. As we focus on Almighty God and the needs of others in the world, we are reminded that our calling in Christ is to serve.

Praise can alleviate stress in a remarkable way, and anger and bitterness have to go too.

Praise can deal with various weaknesses in our lives as we overcome in Christ, and doubts and uncertainty go too when we praise.

We do not need to understand everything when we praise Almighty God because we will trust Him to supply what we require. There will be that knowing that God is in control. Praise the living God and experience it for yourself.

Worship is never about me, or us. It is all about Almighty God. That perspective deals with many emotional needs.

Then, the writer asks for prayer. To ask for a prayer is never a weakness. Pray for us that we may live a consistent life, and the writer wanted to be restored to these disciples quickly.

Verses 20 and 21 of Hebrews Chapter 13 are most moving. They teach us that it has got to be God working in you. Let Him do things in you and through you. Trust Him to do it. He wants to equip us so that we can do His Will. Let Jesus do good through you. God never calls us without equipping us for the task.

We are called to mend what is broken and to make up what is lacking, bringing into harmony what is out of harmony.

It is the God of peace who does this. There is so much to do; the writer is virtually saying, "Jesus, You do it for us."

There are personal greetings at the end and a bit of news. He refers to his short letter. Well, it is. It can be read in an hour. Do take the time to read it. There is always a very real blessing for those who read and study the Word of God.

We do not know the details of this mention that Timothy has been set free, but it is significant.

Greet people. Greeting people can be part of sharing the grace of God. It looks as though the writer was in Rome, but wherever he was, he wanted the grace of Jesus to be with them all. He wanted the grace of the risen and living Lord Jesus Christ to be with all those believers.

# How Does Our Spirituality and Concern Compare With That of This New Testament Leader

The love, concerns, and compassion which this man had in his heart for others caused him at times much hurt and pain and distress.

Caring hearts can be deeply wounded hearts.

Recently, in my reading and study of Paul's first letter to the disciples of Jesus Christ at Thessalonica, I saw these valuable and precious lessons.

Paul would have told them about the cross, and the carrying of the cross of Christ, but it can be one thing to hear about it and another thing to experience it in our lives. He had spent rather a brief time with them because of persecution, but he would have laid a sound foundation. He always did no matter where he went.

Now, these believers in Jesus were having a difficult time. That is one of the reasons why he writes this very personal and rather a powerful letter.

He did not want ongoing affliction to have a negative effect on their faith.

We are called to follow Jesus Christ which inescapably involves suffering, but God can use that suffering for His glory. He did not want these believers to become shaken in their faith by the pressures of persecution and affliction.

Do take the time to read this amazing letter. These findings flow from Chapter 3.

This was part of their basic and elementary teaching, and Paul helps people face it.

Conversion is never the end of the matter. Paul was concerned not simply in having converts but in making disciples, and this is how we can examine our own personal situations in the light of the Word.

It was the Word that made them what they were, and the same Word will do the same for us.

In this letter we see something of Paul's intense love of people and how he cared for their welfare and well-being.

It would be intolerable for him not to know how they were getting on in these dangerous and hazardous circumstances. He was so human and this insight permits us to see a deep concern flowing from a caring heart.

This is Christian love in its simplest form.

He was prepared to be alone in Athens if only he could get news of how these young disciples were getting on back in Thessalonica and he would be equally concerned about those whom he had left in Philippi too.

He had two main aims in his ministry which stretched over some 25 years or so. He had to hold in tension these two goals and tasks. Not only he was concerned about preaching the Gospel and seeing men and women come to faith in Jesus Christ but he was also deeply interested in seeing these believers being built up in the faith.

Now, this is true genuine profound spirituality.

How does our spirituality compare with that of this New Testament leader?

It can be valuable to take the time to evaluate how serious and genuine our faith is and how committed we are to our calling.

# How to Attain Victory in Spiritual Warfare

If spiritual warfare is what things have come down to, then we have already chosen the path of Christ and are now in conflict with the fears of this world. Spiritual warfare is a battle between the carnal man and the spiritual man in us. The most important aspect to remember here is that this war is not in the world but within us. It is not what is outside of us that can harm us. The attack on our person that leads to death is not an attack on our spirit. This is death in the flesh, and we are not accountable for this before God. If we are abused or humiliated by others, it is still not an attack on our spirit but on the flesh. What is of paramount importance is how we react in response to these attacks. Below are simple ways of understanding spiritual warfare and how to overcome our carnal adversary.

**Body**
One of the first points of attack in spiritual warfare is the body. This attack is on our person, it is how we appear to others. Whether it is our looks, our demeanor, our words, or our personality, there is something we shall see about us that we do not like. Our carnal selves demand change and show us what is acceptable in the world. It shows us what appears to be better than us, and before long, we revert to envy. If we believe that God created all things, then we turn to God and ask why we do not have what others have. This is not the world attacking us, this is us attacking us. The world will always be the way it is. God has said that He would let believers and none believers exist until the end of time before Christ returns for judgment. There is no point in worrying about vanity. It is a part of us, and it is something we all have to live with. Winning this battle is in small measures, and ensuring victory is making sure that this vanity does not control our lives.

**Beliefs**

In this dominion, we are questioned about our faith in God and in our Lord and Savior Jesus Christ. God's word is used against us. It is interpreted in many ways for us to see flaws in the human perspective. Again, although this appears to be an external attack from men, the reality is that it is internal. This is to see whether we truly believe in God. If our faith is weak and our belief has no depth, then we would end up questioning it. In this situation, we should not feel that we have to respond in a certain way to win this battle. It is not what man sees or judges us upon that determine our beliefs. It is our conscience before God. We will not always have all the right answers. We will not always have the time or the wisdom to overcome these attacks. However, we can have the faith to realize that no one can take away our belief in God if He has chosen us. A victory here should come from within when we realize that nothing anyone says makes a difference to our faith in God.

**Loyalty**

This is the contest between our faith and love for God and our loyalty to people we love. The decision here is whether we are willing to choose over these people when the circumstance presents itself. What will we gain in answering to God as opposed to a man is the most important thing to consider here. If we choose a man, then we may get love in return from our family and friends, the question is how long this last and when tough times come how do we turn again to God. If we answer to God, then even if we are rebuked by our family, God has the power to convince them to still love and follow us because we chose him in the first place. It is clear here that to win this spiritual battle, we must always choose God first.

**Goliath**

Goliath, in this case, is all our fears. Whether it is in the simplest of things, a job interview, starting a relationship, illness, or any other thing that looks like an impossible task to defeat, it all adds up to fear within us. The key to defeating Goliath lies in the words, "greater is he that is within me than he that is in the world." We must always remember these words because if God is within us, then we can make the impossible possible. This requires constant prayer and a realization that God fights for us from within. The Goliath we are afraid to confront externally is not the problem. The Goliath we are afraid to confront is within us and called fear.

## Our Lord and Savior Jesus Christ

Many would come to us and say that they believe in God but not in his Christ. This should change nothing within us. The thing to remember here is that without Christ we will not understand scripture. He is the savior of mankind whether he is accepted or not. It is through him that we accept the Word of God, and it is only by him that we can reach God. Here it is not so important that we convince others of our beliefs. What is important is that we know within ourselves that he is our Lord and Savior.

Spiritual warfare is not about what we see or what people say. These would never change, and we should not expect it to. Spiritual warfare is about the carnal man versus the spiritual man, and we must recognize that strength in one is a weakness in the other.

# Choices Change Our Lives

W e have all heard the truth that we can choose our actions, but we cannot choose the consequences.

We have all heard that no one else can choose for us. No one can force us to do anything. Our choices are always our choices and what we do or become is up to us.

We know that we choose all the time, and not making a choice is making a choice. Life demands of us that we choose, and if we do not actively make a choice, that is a choice.

Regarding choices, those choices we just made have seem to follow us around for the rest of our lives and this is what I have been thinking about for some time Our choices are not always so important that we notice them tagging us, but they do. Cause and effect mean that everything we choose and everything we do has consequences. Every consequence of our choices and our actions changes our lives. Sometimes almost imperceptibly, sometimes in major ways.

If we make poor choices, we can make better ones in the future to try to negate the poor choices as much as possible, but we can never change the past, and we can never completely negate our past choices.

I am aware that many people have passive attitudes about choices. If they make a poor choice, they think that they can just make another choice and fix it. So what is the big problem? The further we get into an erroneous territory, the harder it is to go back around and swim against the forceful current to reach the neutral territory that we always wanted to attain. Poor choices lead to poor choices. Stupidity leads to stupidity. Failure leads to failure. And of course, success leads to success. Intelligence leads to more intelligence.

And there are people who purposely make poor choices because it seems something they want at the time, thinking that they will enjoy their choices for a while and then will fix the problems with other choices. We hear smokers, and drug addicts say that they can quit anytime they want. Experience seems the opposite.

I heard about some young people who were taught all their lives that it was important not to have a premarital sex. So they went off to Las Vegas, got married to people they felt no love or commitment for, had sex, and then got divorced—all within one weekend, if memory serves. Apparently, in their minds, that was okay because they did not have an extra-marital sex. To people who have fully developed judgment, that is crazy. That was a poor choice. In this case, getting married did not make the sex any less illicit. They might as well have saved the money it cost to travel to Las Vegas. That choice and those actions will follow them around for the rest of their lives. They can learn from it, they can teach others not to do what they did, they can make sure that their present and future are better, but they can never get away from what they did.

Sometimes we wish our past would go away and leave us alone. It cannot. It should not. Our past will always stick around so that we can learn from it and can reminisce each consequence of having both good and bad choices we have made. Then we are equipped to make better choices in the future. Many times my past comes up out of nowhere and embarrasses me. No one else knows, and often, even other people who were involved at the time mercifully do not remember anything about it.

Remembering the pain and embarrassment of some of the things from our past and determining to live a better life because of them produce wisdom. Wisdom is the ability to make better choices because of having made poor choices or because of having seen the consequences of others' poor choices.

Also, sometimes, good choices I have made come back to me and surprise me in pleasant ways. They reminded me of how it feels to have chosen and acted in the right ways. They helped me in my determination to keep on continuing to make good choices, as much as I possibly can, right now and for the rest of my life. They contribute to my wisdom also. I understand choices and consequences from having made both good and bad choices and from having done both good and bad things. I prefer to get any wisdom I can by learning from my good choices.

# Change With Your Brain in Mind

Making a decision to begin paying attention to something different, something new, and something that may be uncomfortable, in effect, can make a change in your life if you want to. Attending to something new generates new experiences, which can eventually drive different results.

Making a positive change in your life is first about focusing your attention on new experiences.

But anyone who has attempted to change her or his life knows how hard it is. I have written about the importance of meaningful experiences to overcome the fear, doubt, and procrastination that we all have to deal with.

What I have not written about yet is that there is also a physical aspect to why it is so difficult to change: our brains do not want to.

As humans beings, our five senses bring us a continuous stream of information. We are constantly in some combination of hearing, seeing, tasting, touching, and smelling our environment.

However, because of the way the brain works, most of what our senses take in never makes it to conscious awareness.

How your brain is "wired" is a complicated subject, but I want to touch on it briefly to bring to your attention (no pun intended) on the important fundamentals about your brain that influences your behavior and how your brain responds to change.

First, your brain is the largest consumer of energy in your body. When you are focused on something, your brain is consuming a tremendous amount of energy.

Second, because humans evolved in a world where energy was scarce and you did not always know where your next meal was coming from, conserving energy evolved as a fundamental survival principle.

Third, as the largest consumer of energy, your brain evolved to conserve energy wherever possible. One of the ways the brain conserves energy is discarding if you will; inputs from your senses that your brain has previously identified as non-threatening or routine.

Fourth, ignoring or paying little attention to previously identified sounds, sights, etc. allows your brain to be ready to pay attention to things that are new and potentially food, or something that sees you as food. Remember 50,000 years ago that you did not necessarily know where your next meal was coming from, but equally important you did not necessarily know when you would encounter something that wanted to make you their next meal.

So in order to be able to quickly recognize a threat in your environment and to conserve energy, your brain wants to be in stable, well-known places. For example, your brain wants the sounds it hears to be routine, repetitive sounds it hears every day, so it can be ready to attend to unusual noises like a lion's roar or someone approaching. As an interesting side, our brains are wired so that loud noises go directly to the part of the brain that controls the fight or flight response, which is why we jump at loud noises, even sometimes when we know they are coming.

Because focused attention increases the already large amount of energy your brain consumes, your brain is also hard-wired to quickly incorporate the new and the novel into the common and routine. Continuing our examples of sound, have you ever noticed how people who have lived next to a railroad or subway for a long time seem to barely notice the train roaring by? How they get up to steady a plate about to vibrate off the table all the while continuing their conversation without pause or even looking at the passing train; just automatically raising their voices so they can be heard, while you are totally focused on how loud the train is.

One of the ways our brains help us to reduce how much we have to pay attention to things is through habits. Once you have a routine down in the morning, you do not really think about it. You are probably thinking about something else while you go through the motions of what you do every morning.

This can be true of even complex tasks. Think about how much attention and focus it required when you were learning how to drive a car and how soon the act of driving no longer dominated your attention. You might have probably heard of someone saying, or maybe you have said this yourself, "I don't mind the long drive into work. It gives me more time to think about what I have to get done that day."

Or think about those first few days for a new job or a new school when everything was new and unusual and how much conscious thought and effort it took while you made your way to a new environment. Then contrast that with what it is like today now that the environment is no longer new and getting to work, or school is routine. Then think about how annoyed you get when something takes you out of your routine.

Becoming accustomed to our environment happens naturally. You do not decide; it just happens.

Your brain wants to free up your conscious mind from routine events, avoiding the energy drain they would cause, so that you are ready to attend to the unusual, the important, the life threatening, or life sustaining.

The important point here is that your brain has evolved over time to classify much of what you experience every day into non-important routine events that do not require a lot of attention so that you are free to attend to new or important experiences.

However, just because the brain wants to make sure you can attend to new events does not mean it likes the new or the novel. In fact, it is just the opposite, which we will explore next.

Once you have desired to make a change in your life, you are in effect making a decision to begin paying attention to something different, something new, and something that may be uncomfortable and quite challenging.

There are three important points here.

One, your brain does not want new; it wants the familiar, the low energy experiences that it knows and feels safe about.

Two, your brain is going to compare new experiences with what it knows and look to avoid repeating the experience, especially if your conscious mind thinks of the new experience as negative.

Third, in spite of point number 2, if the experience is repeated enough, it begins to incorporate that experience, even negative ones, into the familiar so that it does not burn up so much energy.

When you have the desire to make a change in your life, remember that your brain is wired not to like any changes. The status quo is safe. Change is risky and takes energy. Your brain wants to conserve all of your energy. The brain wants certainty. Change is uncertain.

Of course, I do not mean to say that change is impossible. Obviously, it is. However, whenever I talk to someone about a change that they have always wanted to make in their life, I often talk to them about the way our brains are wired.

As an overprotective relative or friend who gets anxious when you want to do something new, our brains will experience discomfort with the new changes.

So knowing that, are there ways you can help your brain and yourself get beyond the threatening, energy intensive new to a place where change becomes the safe low energy familiar?

The answer is yes, and I am going to touch on the seven ways that you can align your thoughts and actions with how your brain works.

(1) Expectation—Set your expectations to what you want to experience in the world and you will notice more of it.

Have you ever noticed how after you decided to buy a new electronic device or maybe a new car, you suddenly get the feeling and begin to see them everywhere?

They did not magically appear. They were always there. However, you tend not to notice things unrelated to your interests.

What changed is related to how making a decision to do something acts on your perceptual processes. It affects how neurons fire in response to what we see. The object of your decision now has your interest, and the perceptual part of your brain starts to respond when it recognizes something related to your new interest.

Instead of the "nothing to see here, let us move on" type of response that may not even make it your conscious awareness, your brain responds with a "hey there has been some interest here, better send it up to have it checked out."

Things we may see or hear about real estate investing may barely register in our conscious awareness until we decide we are interested in real estate investing.

In addition to paying more attention to real estate investing, your brain will automatically begin to compare and contrast this new interest with previous experiences looking for something familiar.

Your brain uses previous experience to set expectations for what your perceptual circuits should be looking for to send up to our conscious awareness. Expectations alter how you experience events. Your inner expectations influence what information you take notice of in the world.

When the expectation is negative, your brain primes itself to sense evidence of negative outcomes. Once primed your brain will focus on every hint of the negative, real or imagined, and ignore or minimize the positive.

You can prepare the perceptual part of your brain by where you direct your attention.

Set your expectations to what you want to experience in the world, and you will notice more of it. Repetition and Goals can help you get your expectations focused in the right direction.

(2) Repetition—The more you do something, the less energy your brain needs to do it.

Making a change, from something simple like shopping in a new grocery store to learning a musical instrument, is a process of making new connections in your brain.

Various neural patterns in different parts of the brain begin to make a connection once you learn new skills and/or tasks. The more times a task is being repeated, the stronger those connections will become. The stronger that they become, the more automatic the task becomes and is easily done, reducing the energy needed for our conscious awareness (think to learn to drive a car).

Remember your brain wants to automate as much of what it does as possible so it can be free to pay attention to changes in your environment that may represent a threat.

Simple tasks can become automatic in as little as three repetitions; however, complex tasks may take many hours. Highly complex tasks, like developing expertise in some endeavor, are an ongoing process that requires several thousands of hours of practice and reflection.

The kind of change you are contemplating or trying to make is likely of the more complex variety, and you can easily become overwhelmed by it. That is where the right goals can help.

(3) Goals—Make the complex a lot of samples.

To help make things more automatic, complex learning tasks are better when they are divided into smaller, more manageable portions.

Change that is divided into a sequence of smaller, simpler tasks is less likely to cause stress from uncertainty, fear, or ambiguity and thus increase your chances of success.

Our brains are wired to immediately detect changes or possible errors in the environment and to send strong signals to alert us to anything unusual, or unknown. This alert error mechanism in the brain is closely connected to the brain's fear circuitry. Error detection causes us to act more emotionally and more impulsively.

Our thinking can be easily overwhelmed and flooded with error signals when we are faced with situations of uncertainty, rejection, unfairness, or ambiguity.

To use learning to drive as an example, most of us started slowly someplace where there is little traffic. Our brain was busily making new connections between the parts of the brain that handle vision, motor controls, and making decisions. The increasing level of comfort you felt as you learned to drive was a result of the increasingly stronger connections developing within your brain.

Imagine how your brain would respond if, for your first driving lesson, your driving instructor drove you on the ramp of a busy fast-moving eight-lane freeway and told you to take the driver's seat, get on the freeway, and immediately get into the fast lane.

Sometimes in our zeal for self-improvement and personal development, we in effect try to jump right into the fast lane.

Set smaller goals that are specific and well defined, so you know what action to take. You will also have more success with goals that are time defined instead of vague references to the future: two months as opposed to sometime next year. They should be measurable, so you can track your progress and challenge enough to provide a level of engagement but not so challenging as to produce stress and invoke error signals.

Breaking down large tasks into smaller portions also helps you to leverage Expectation and Repetition. By taking incremental steps, you can leverage the brain's desire to automate tasks. As you build your expertise, your brain is developing the connections that allow the brain to perform functions related to your new skills in a less stressful, lower energy, more automated fashion.

The brain also uses past experiences to set expectations for future events. The brains experience of success through gradual steps helps set the expectation for more success which primes your perceptual system to look for confirmations of future success, not confirmations of past failure.

Setting the right goals can help you create and sustain the belief that you can succeed, but you also need time to focus.

(4) Focus—Make the most of the limited time you have.

Your conscious awareness and the brain circuits that support it are easily distracted by the endless incoming sensory inputs that your brain is processing. It requires immense energy to maintain your focus on just one thing.

Distraction is a signal that something in your environment has changed and that you have to pay attention to it. The key phrase here is "have to." Attending to change signals in the environment is automatic. Your brain is hard wired to alert you to anything that might be a threat.

Focus is much easier in environments where you can tune out distractions. For some, this will be a quiet place, but for others, silence is in itself a distraction, and they focus best in an open, public place like a coffee shop.

When you focus on a single task, you are making deeper connections within your brain. Focus helps move what you are learning into long-term memory, so it can be more easily retrieved when needed.

Research has shown that your peak period for focused work is only one to two hours per day. If those hours are in an environment where you are constantly being distracted, you are wasting valuable time. Our peak time of day also tends to be either early in the morning or late at night. Find the best time for you.

(5) Visualization—Seeing is connecting.

The circuitry of the brain that is used to do physically something has the same pathways used when we imagine it. Real and imagined events are not distinguished.

Rehearsing mentally can prepare mental circuits in ways similar to actually doing something. Visualization can also help to resolve fears when you "see" yourself making the change or doing the tasks you want to accomplish. Visualization also leverages the power of repetition to build and strengthen neural connections.

There are three important aspects of visualization.

First, it has to be correct. Visualizing something incorrectly only serves to strengthen incorrect behavior.

Second, the more vivid and detailed you can make the visualization, the more connections it creates in the brain.

Third, visualization is most effective in short durations spaced over time. It is better to spend 3 minutes a day for 5 days rather than visualizing something for 20 minutes in one day.

(6) Social Connections—Connecting with people builds connections in your brain.

Some have written that time spent connecting with others is more important than even maintaining a good diet.

As humans, we are first and foremost social beings. The brain rewards us when we make quality social connections. When we connect with others in a mutual exchange of sharing emotions, goals, and ideas, the brain releases oxytocin, a chemical that gives us a great sense of pleasure.

Find others who share your interest in the change you want to make. Seek out those, who like you, have set out to change their life, to learn a new skill, to start a new business, or to start a new chapter in their lives. Sharing your experiences and listening to others share their experiences helps your brain moderate its perception of the change as a threat.

These rewards further strengthen the connections you are building in your brain and provide a positive motivation to continue. Learners are most motivated when they possess the belief that they can succeed at learning.

(7) Downtime—Give yourself a break.

Finally, one activity we all need is sufficient time to refresh our brains. Make sure to spend some time being non-goal focused. Like your muscles after exercise, our neural circuits benefit from a period of recovery.

Quiet time is also an important factor in solving complex problems. When we are constantly attending to the electronic imperatives of computers and mobile devices, our conscious brain can be too busy to notice the solutions our quieter, the subconscious is sending up to us. Too much constant on the go and you miss the "Aha!" moments that pop into your thoughts when you are not thinking about anything in particular.

As you work toward what success means to you, be mindful of your expectations, that repetition helps your brain automate change, and that splitting change into smaller pieces helps avoid getting overwhelmed. Focus is valuable but limited, so do not waste it; visualization is real to the brain; quality social connections are rewarded; and downtime gives us time to listen to our subconscious.

# Conclusion

PAIN DEFINED. Catching up with a friend recently brought the added surprise that she had undergone extensive shoulder surgery. Replete with this very elaborate but uncomfortable looking brace she explained the lengthy process of recovery, including pain management during the initial stages and how important it is post-operatively.

Having never undergone any major surgery myself, the issue of post-operative pain management was a relatively new thing for me. The principle is this: if the patient is in pain, they will be tense. Simplistically, tense musculature and other tissues will not readily release their toxins or facilitate rejuvenating blood flow, etc., and recovery is therefore slowed.

Therefore, therapeutic pain management is crucial in post-operative recovery and care.

As my friend spoke, I instantly thought how similar this is to the issue of spiritual healing and how unreconciled emotional, and hence, mental pain would be almost always slow and even stunt the spiritual healing of a person. And then, of course, I thought of the reverse; that the miraculous spiritual healing of God would aid mental and emotional healing—a more holistic healing.

"Pain management" as far as mental and emotional pain is concerned must be about having the moral courage and strength (Joshua 1: 9) to deal with emotional baggage promptly and adequately or, at the very least, deal with it at some point.

If we do not learn to manage this pain in our lives, our spiritual recovery is stunted, and our growth and potential are delayed.

Just because mental and emotional pain can be covered over by a veneer of life choice and comforts does not mean it is not there. Like paracetamol, the things we do to make the pain more bearable purely mask the pain, never dealing with the cause.

The purpose of paracetamol is simply to help us cope with a temporary pain—pain that will resolve itself—i.e., a headache or stomach ache, etc. It is, however, no good for the person who is suffering chronic (ongoing) pain. They will need a more invasive intervention. And so it is for mental and emotional pain; most often we must have a remedy that addresses the cause.

Flipping this on its head then, we have the case of Christ, as far as Spiritual healing augmenting the mental and emotional realms of dysfunction are concerned.

Nothing is beyond the Spirit of God. Miracles are His business—the "stock in trade."

Would it be surprising to learn that God has all the answers to all your mental and emotional pain?—not only just some of it but also all of it. At a level beyond our understanding—proving it to be miraculous—He attends to the meaning of the pain. We still have the pain, but it means less, and it is less limiting; indeed, we can then triumph over the pain. Little by little the meaning is taken from the pain. And at some point, the pain is all gone, but the appreciation of it remains—we honor the pain. It becomes a triumphant marker of whom we are and who we have become.

Thank you for downloading this book. I hope that it has answered all your questions on Emotions and will benefit you even as you apply it to your life.

---

Finally, if you have enjoyed this book, then I'd like to ask for a favour, would you be kind enough to leave a review for this book on Amazon?, It'd be greatly appreciated!

To receive free updates on further releases from Felix and other related material from Evoque Publishing please sign up at the following Url: www.evoquepublishing.com/signup